Country File
Italy

Ian Graham

A⁺
Smart Apple Media

First published in 2004 by Franklin Watts
96 Leonard Street, London EC2A 4XD, UK

Franklin Watts Australia
45–51 Huntley Street, Alexandria, NSW 2015

Country File: Italy produced for Franklin Watts by Bender
Richardson White, PO Box 266, Uxbridge, UK.

Editor: Lionel Bender, *Designer and Page Make-up:* Ben
White, *Picture Researcher:* Cathy Stastny, *Cover Make-up:*
Mike Pilley, Radius, *Production:* Kim Richardson, *Graphics
and Maps:* Stefan Chabluk

Copyright © 2004 Bender Richardson White

Consultant: Dr. Terry Jennings, a former teacher and
university lecturer. He is now a full-time writer of children's
geography and science books.

Published in the United States by Smart Apple Media
1980 Lookout Drive, North Mankato, Minnesota 56003

Library of Congress Control Number: 2004100040

ISBN 1-58340-497-X

9 8 7 6 5 4 3 2 1

The Author
Ian Graham is a full-time writer and
editor of nonfiction books. He has
written more than 100 books for
young readers.

Contents

Welcome to Italy 4

The Land 6

The People 8

Urban and Rural Life 10

Farming and Fishing 12

Resources and Industry 14

Transportation 16

Education 18

Sports and Leisure 20

Daily Life and Religion 22

Arts and Media 24

Government 26

Place in the World 28

Database 30

Glossary 31

Index 32

Welcome to Italy

The Republic of Italy, usually known simply as Italy, is located in southern Europe. It is a peninsula, or projection of land, stretching out into the Mediterranean Sea in the shape of a long boot with the island of Sicily at its toe.

Italy is slightly larger than the state of Arizona and is more than three times the size of Great Britain. In addition to the Italian mainland, it includes several islands, among them Sicily and Sardinia, the two largest islands in the Mediterranean. Italy is known for its rich history, mild climate, fashionable clothes, art, and distinctive food—based on pasta, tomatoes, olives, and wine. Italian cheeses and ice cream are delicacies in many countries, too.

DATABASE

Neighbors, states, and regions

Italy is surrounded on three sides by sea. Its 1,240-mile (2,000 km) land boundary is shared with Vatican City and five countries—Austria, France, San Marino, Slovenia, and Switzerland. San Marino and Vatican City, home to the Pope, are completely enclosed by Italy.

Italy was divided into many small states until 1861. The states developed their own identities and customs, many of which survive to the present time and give modern Italy its strong regional character, trade, and tourism.

Florence, an important historic city, is situated on the river Arno. ▼

The Land

I taly is a very mountainous and hilly country. It is located where two great plates of Earth's crust meet, which produces occasional volcanic eruptions and earthquakes.

There are two main mountain ranges on Italy's mainland—the Alps and the Apennines. The Alps run from east to west along the northern border and spill over into neighboring countries. They contain some of Europe's highest mountains, including Monte Bianco (also known as Mont Blanc) and Monte Cervino (also known as the Matterhorn). The eastern end of the Alps includes the Dolomites. The Apennines run the length of the country.

The town of San Gimignano lies in the northern region of Tuscany. The Tuscan landscape of rolling hills, cypress trees, and small farms is featured in many historic Italian paintings. ▶▶

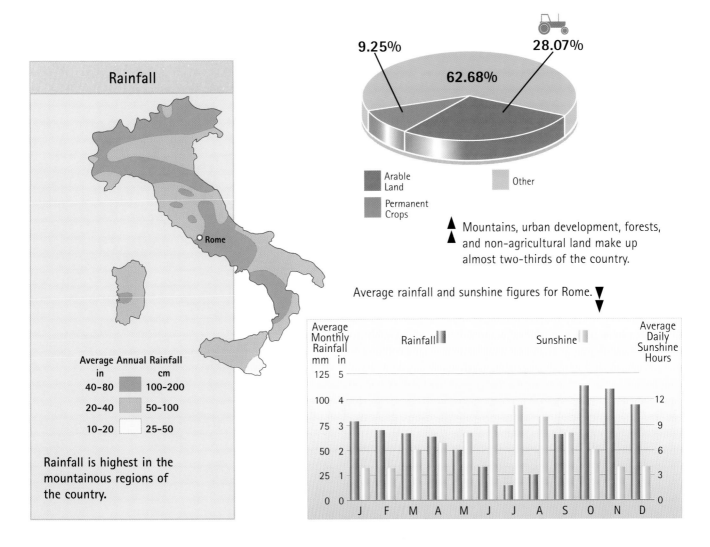

Rainfall

Average Annual Rainfall

in	cm
40–80	100–200
20–40	50–100
10–20	25–50

Rainfall is highest in the mountainous regions of the country.

9.25%

62.68%

28.07%

Arable Land

Permanent Crops

Other

▲▲ Mountains, urban development, forests, and non-agricultural land make up almost two-thirds of the country.

Average rainfall and sunshine figures for Rome. ▼▼

Average Monthly Rainfall mm in — Rainfall — Sunshine — Average Daily Sunshine Hours

J F M A M J J A S O N D

Volcanoes and ancient sea bed

Most of Italy's rivers begin in the Apennines. The longest is the Po. Some of Italy's lakes are flooded valleys that were carved out of the ground by glaciers. Others are flooded volcano craters. Italy has several active volcanoes, including Vesuvius, Etna, and Stromboli. It was an eruption of Mount Vesuvius in A.D. 79 that destroyed the ancient Roman cities of Pompeii and Herculaneum, burying them in ash.

The largest expanse of flat land in Italy is the Po Valley, the land surrounding the river Po. It was once part of the Adriatic Sea, the arm of the Mediterranean Sea that borders Italy's east coast. Over millions of years, the area gradually filled with mud, sand, and silt that washed down from the mountains and became dry land.

Climate

Italy's climate is mild because most of its landmass is surrounded by warm Mediterranean waters. The hottest month is July and the coldest is January. The wettest is October and the driest is July. The summers are generally warm and dry around the coasts and cooler in the mountains. Winters are milder in the south than in the north.

The People

People have lived in the land of Italy for hundreds of thousands of years. Today, the population is about 57.4 million. Most people live in the prosperous northern half of the country.

During Italy's long history, it has been invaded and settled by many different peoples from other parts of Europe and the Mediterranean. Their different cultures and influences have merged together to form the Italian people of today. The average age of the population is rising, as in many Western countries, because the birth rate is falling. Italy was the first country in the world to have more people over the age of 65 than under the age of 15.

Italians buy cheese from a market stall in Siena, a town in the central region of Italy. There, many people have ancestors from France, Germany, and Switzerland. ▼

Language

The Italian language as we know it today has existed only since the country was unified. Until then, Italian was spoken differently in various regions. Some of the old dialects are still spoken at home in some places and within small communities. Near the northern borders, people often speak the language of the adjacent country.

A changing population

Italy has been a country of emigration since the beginning of the 18th century. Many people left because of poverty, especially in southern Italy. They also fled from the hardships of World War I and the later fascism that overtook Italy in the 1930s. Most settled in other European countries and North America.

Since the mid-1970s, immigration has increased as Italians have begun to return home in larger numbers, and more people have also arrived from poorer countries such as Albania, Bosnia, and Herzegovina.

 Shoppers in Rome, where Italians speak with a distinct Mediterranean lilt.

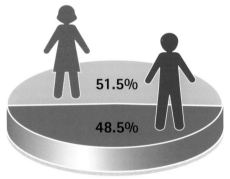

51.5%

48.5%

Female Population
29,578,000

Male Population
27,845,000

▲ There are more women than men in the Italian population.

:::::::::::::::::::::: **DATABASE** ::::::::::::::::::::::

Ancient history

The earliest evidence of human settlement in Italy was found in Isernia, southeast of Rome, and was dated to about 730,000 years ago. Another site near Verona is more than 400,000 years old. They are among the oldest human settlements in Europe. Remains of more recent prehistoric human settlements are found all across Italy.

 Web Search ►►

► http://www.cia.gov/cia/
publications/factbook/
geos/it.html
The CIA World Factbook entry on Italy and its people, government, and economy.

9

Urban and Rural Life

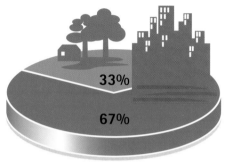

33%

67%

■ Percentage of Population
Living in Urban Areas

■ Percentage of Population
Living in Rural Areas

About two-thirds of Italians live in
towns and cities.

Venice

Venice is a unique city. It is
built on 118 islands that are
linked by bridges. Instead of
roads and cars, its thorough-
fares are canals, and its traffic
is watercraft (see cover photo).
Its population of about
280,000 is overwhelmed by
more than 10 million tourists
every year.

Italians meet on a street in Bolzano, a
town in Trentino-Alto Adige in the far
north of the country. This mountainous
region of Italy has many small towns
and villages but no large cities. ►►

The difference between urban and rural life in Italy
is not as dramatic as in many other countries.
Many of Italy's towns and cities—most of which are in
the north of the country—have retained much of their
traditional charm and relaxed pace of life.

Italy's biggest cities, including Rome, the capital, have
their share of modern buildings, but they are not the
concrete and glass cityscapes found elsewhere in Europe.
Industrialization came to Italy later than to other European
countries, so the red-tiled roofs and cobbled piazzas of its
old cities were not swept away in massive commercial and
industrial redevelopments. One exception is Milan. Italy's
economic powerhouse is more like London or Paris. Life in
Milan is as fast and hectic as in any city anywhere.

◄◄ Farm workers gather olives in an olive grove in Puglia, a southern rural area that forms the "heel" of Italy.

Population

Most Italians live in the flatter and more fertile north of the country.

○ Rome

Persons per	
square mile	square km
Less than 2.5	Less than 1
2.5–25	1–10
25–250	10–100
250–500	100–200
Over 500	over 200

The capital city

Rome is a special city. Once the most powerful city on Earth, its citizens still take great pride in being Romans. To live in Rome is to live surrounded by 2,000 years of history. The Colosseum, a great amphitheater that opened in A.D. 80 and is still a major landmark in Rome today, was once the scene of savage combat between gladiators.

Rural life

In rural areas, people often follow a more traditional way of life. They are more likely to live in a close-knit family with as many as three generations under the same roof. Their houses are typically grouped together in a village on a hilltop or among farmland. Each village has a small church and a marketplace. The peaceful surroundings, beautiful countryside, good food, and mild weather of rural areas—including Tuscany and Umbria—make them favorite destinations for tourists seeking a relaxing break.

Web Search ►►

► http://www.initaly.com/regions/umbria/umbria.htm
Web site of the Umbria region.

Farming and Fishing

Italy's mountainous land makes much of the country unsuitable for farming. Despite this, Italy is almost self-sufficient in food.

The northern part of Italy concentrates mainly on the production of cereals, sugarbeets, soy beans, meat, and dairy products. The southern part, with its milder climate, specializes more in fruit, vegetables, olive oil, wine, and durum wheat. Wheat and rice are also grown in the fertile Po Valley. Most Italian farms are small, and many of them have been owned and run by the same families for generations. Large quantities of citrus fruits, olives, olive oil, tomatoes, and wine are exported. Italy is the world's leading producer of wine.

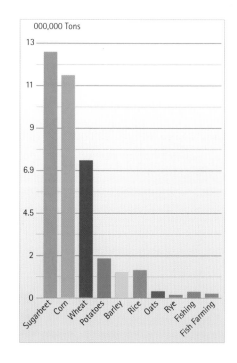

000,000 Tons

A comparison by weight of the annual production of major crops and the fishing industry in Italy. ►►

Farming Regions

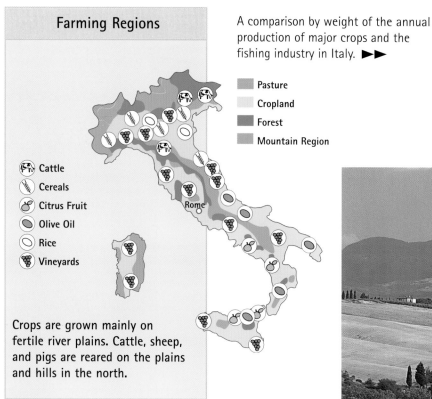

Pasture
Cropland
Forest
Mountain Region

Rome

🐄 Cattle
🌾 Cereals
🍊 Citrus Fruit
🫒 Olive Oil
🍚 Rice
🍇 Vineyards

Crops are grown mainly on fertile river plains. Cattle, sheep, and pigs are reared on the plains and hills in the north.

A view of wheatfields in Tuscany after the harvest. Tuscany is a major agricultural region and central Italy's most important winemaking area. ▼

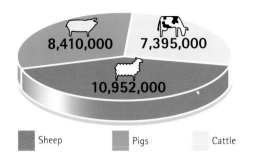

8,410,000   7,395,000

10,952,000

Sheep   Pigs   Cattle

▲ A comparison of the numbers of livestock raised in Italy. Chickens, geese, and goats are also raised on farms.

Commercial fishing

Italy has a fishing fleet of about 19,000 boats—almost one-fifth of the entire European Union fishing fleet of 100,000 boats. The sea around Italy is divided into three areas—the west coast (Tyrrhenian Sea), the east coast (Adriatic Sea), and the islands (Sicily and Sardinia). The Adriatic fleet is the largest. The total fishing catch, including deep-sea trawling, fish farming, and mussel and oyster beds, is more than half a million tons per year.

Parma specialities

Farms around the town of Parma in central Italy produce two of Italy's culinary delicacies—Parma ham and parmesan cheese. The hard cheese, which is aged for at least two years and is delicious grated over meals, is also important in the production of the ham. The delicately cured meat comes from pigs fattened on whey, a watery liquid left over from making the cheese.

▲ Small fishing boats at the dockside in Palermo, Sicily. These boats make short trips and small catches each day. Deep-sea trawlers spend many days at sea before returning to the docks to unload their huge catches.

Web Search ▶▶

▶ http://www.italyemb.org /AGRICULTURE.htm
Information from the Italian embassy in the U.S. about agriculture in Italy.

13

Resources and Industry

Italy's economy changed dramatically after the end of World War II in 1945. It rapidly developed from being based on agriculture into one of the world's largest industrial economies.

Italy has few natural resources. Most of the coal, petroleum, and raw materials that it needs for energy, building, and manufacturing have to be imported. Much of it is brought in by sea. Italy has one of the world's biggest merchant fleets. Natural gas is its most important mineral resource, yielding 24 billion cubic yards (18 billion cu m) a year.

Italy's major industries are tourism, textiles, chemicals, vehicle manufacturing, shipbuilding, iron and steel production, food processing, textiles, and electrical goods. Its manufacturers are mostly located in the northern part of the country. The government's attempts to develop and industrialize the south have met with mixed success.

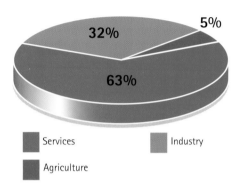

5%
32%
63%

Services
Industry
Agriculture

▲ In recent decades, service industries such as finance, tourism, and business have grown rapidly.

Resources and Industry

⊗ Aerospace
⊖ Car Manufacture
$ Finance
▣ Hi-Tech Industry
⊛ Iron and Steel
▽ Textiles
⚎ Tourism
◇ Salt
▯ Cement
▲ Pumice

Rome

Italy's major industries are concentrated in the north of the country.

▲ Italy is one of the world's biggest producers of marble for use in building and sculpture. It is also a major producer of cement and steel.

 Italy is one of the world's leading designers and manufacturers of high-performance car engines and bodies. A prototype sports car is being assembled above.

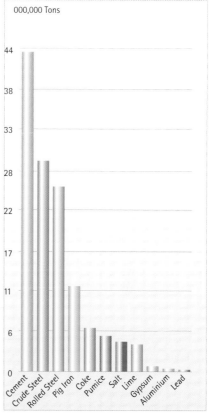

000,000 Tons

 Annual industrial mineral production.

Designer Clothes

Italian fashion is a very successful international business. The stylish designer clothing and accessories, made by fashion houses such as Armani, Versace, Gucci, and Prada are highly sought after around the world.

Web Search ►►

► http://minerals.usgs.gov/ minerals/pubs/country/ 2001/itmyb01.pdf
Information about Italy's minerals industry from the U.S. Geological Survey.

► http://minerals.usgs.gov/ minerals/pubs/country/ maps/94219.gif
A map of Italy's mineral resources from the U.S. Geological Survey.

From small to global companies

Most of Italy's companies are small- or medium-sized, and many of them are family run. In the European Union, companies employ an average of 15 people. The average Italian company employs fewer than four people.

Although there are few large companies, some of them are so internationally successful that they have become household names all over the world. They include the car manufacturers Ferrari, Alfa Romeo, and Fiat, the tire manufacturer Pirelli, and the computer and business machine manufacturer Olivetti.

Transportation

Traveling around Italy is fast and easy because of its extensive road and railroad networks, ferries, and air services. It also has a small network of canals.

Italy's cities are linked by express highways, called autostradas. Most of the autostradas are toll roads. Drivers must pay a fee to use them. Driving in Italy's cities can be difficult because of congestion and frequent traffic jams. Vehicles drive on the right side of the road.

Railroads

After many years of neglect, Italian railroads are going through a period of reform and modernization. Intercity trains are modern, comfortable, and air-conditioned. Local and rural trains often use older rolling stock. Rome and Milan have their own underground railroads, or Metros.

The two main long-distance railroad lines are the Tirrenica, which runs from the French border to Sicily down the west coast, and the Adriatica, which runs from Austria and the former Yugoslavia down the east coast to Taranto. The Pendolino is a luxury service between Milan and Rome. It is expected to be extended to other parts of the country in the future.

Air and sea

Most long-distance international air travelers arrive in Italy at either Rome's Leonardo da Vinci (Fiumicino) Airport or Milan's Malpensa Airport. European flights also arrive at Milan Linate, Naples, Pisa, Turin, and Venice. There are internal flights between most cities.

Italy's ports and offshore islands are served by a large fleet of ferries. Hydrofoils—boats that skim fast over the water—operate on some of the larger lakes and on some routes between the mainland and the islands.

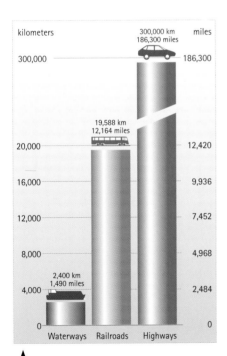

▲ The Italian road network includes more than 3,700 miles (6,000 km) of autostradas (highways).

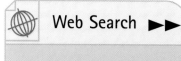

Transportation

The road, rail, and air networks reach all parts of the mainland and major islands.

Major Airports
Major Ports
Highways
Main Roads
Railroads

Venice Trieste Milan Turin Genoa Bologna Firenze Ancona Assisi Rome Fóggia Bari Naples Potenza Brindisi Taranto Palermo Messina Reggio Catania Siracusa Olbia Oristano Cagliari

▲
▲ Modern, high-speed Eurocity trains bring passengers to the heart of Italy from many neighboring countries, such as France, Spain, and Germany.

◄◄ The streets of cities such as Rome are often clogged with buses and cars. Many people use motorscooters to avoid being caught in traffic jams.

Web Search ►►

► http://www.fs-on-line. com
A site that gives information about Italy's state railroads.

► http://www.embitaly.org. uk/general/general_view 20.html
Information about transportation, from the Embassy of Italy in London.

17

Education

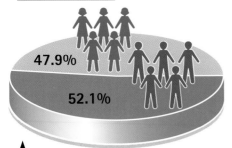

47.9%

52.1%

▲ In pre-elementary (nursery) schools, there is a higher proportion of boys.

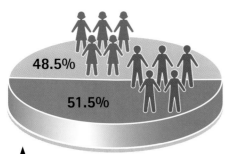

48.5%

51.5%

▲ There is a higher proportion of boys in elementary schools, too.

Montessori Schools

The Italian doctor and educator, Maria Montessori (1870–1952) invented a new way of teaching children with obvious learning difficulties. Instead of traditional blackboard teaching, she encouraged children to use beads and bricks to help focus their attention on simple tasks and develop their manual skills. The system proved so successful that Montessori schools have been set up in many countries and continue to operate today.

Italy has a well-educated population. The literacy rate has risen rapidly to about 98 percent for both men and women. As recently as 1900, it was as low as 30 percent in southern Italy when compared to more than 90 percent in France and Germany at the same time.

Education is mandatory from the age of 6 to 15. It is free of charge at state schools, but some parents pay tuition to send their children to private schools. The school day lasts from 8:30 A.M. to 1:00 P.M. Monday to Saturday, or 8:30 A.M. to 4:30 P.M. Monday to Friday with a one-hour lunch break.

Every year, up to 1.5 million children between the ages of three and five years attend pre-elementary, or nursery, school. About one-quarter of these are private schools. Elementary school begins at the age of six. Children learn a broad range of subjects, including math, science, history, geography, languages, social studies, religious education, art, music, and physical education.

Elementary physical education includes all kinds of sports equipment. ▼
▼

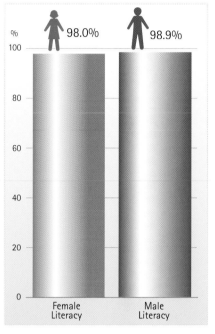

◄◄ At the age of 11, children usually go from elementary to secondary school. In some regions, children between the ages of 8 and 12 attend a middle school before going on to secondary education.

98.0%   98.9%

▲
▲ Literacy is slightly higher among men than women.

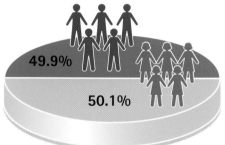

49.9%

50.1%

▲
▲ In secondary schools, girls slightly outnumber boys.

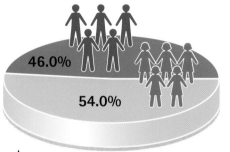

46.0%

54.0%

▲
▲ Girls form a significantly higher proportion of college students.

Secondary and university education

At secondary school, children specialize in classical, scientific, technical, or artistic studies. If they stay in secondary school for five years, they can take an exam for the *Diploma di Maturità* (Matriculation) in their chosen studies. Gaining this diploma grants them admission to college to study for a degree. Students can then, if they wish, go on to study for a more specialized degree or diploma and then a doctorate (a PhD degree).

🌐 Web Search ►►

► http://unstats.un.org/ unsd/demographic/ social/illiteracy.htm
Information about illiteracy for many countries, including Italy, from the United Nations Statistical Division.

Sports and Leisure

Italy is a nation of enthusiastic sports fans. Millions of Italians follow their favorite soccer players, basketball players, race car drivers, and cyclists.

The most popular sport is soccer. Italian teams such as AC Milan, Inter Milan, Juventus, Lazio, Napoli, and Roma attract enormous numbers of spectators for their matches. Italy's national team has won the World Cup three times, in 1934, 1938, and 1982. After soccer, basketball is the next favorite sport.

Italy has a long tradition of making beautiful cars that have enjoyed great success in international motor racing. Italians follow the fortunes of their racing teams and drivers very closely. Ferrari is one of the most successful teams in Formula 1 motor racing.

The modern Olympic stadium in Rome, where international athletics events are held and where both Lazio and Roma soccer clubs play. ▼

Festivals

Numerous festivals and traditional events are held across Italy. Many of them are hundreds of years old. One of the most famous is the Palio in Siena. The Palio is a bareback horse race around the Campo, Siena's historic central square. It has been held since the 13th century and was named after the silk banner presented to the winner. There are modern arts festivals, too. One of the best-known is the Venice Film Festival.

Motor Racing

There are Formula 1 grand prix motor-racing circuits at Monza, near Milan, and at Imola in San Marino. The heart of Italian motor racing is Maranello, near the town of Modena. This is the home and exhibition center of the Ferrari company, where visitors can see some of its vintage and new racing cars.

Bocce

A form of bowling, called *bocce* or *boccia*, has been played in Italy for more than 2,000 years. Players take turns to roll a ball as close as possible to a target ball. The winner is the player who gets the most balls closest to the target. Italian emigrants took bocce to the U.S., where there are now about a million players.

In the summer, Italians and tourists flock to the beaches and holiday resorts along the coast, such as the small town of Camogli in the Liguria region. ▼

Cycling and wintersports

Cycling is very popular, too. The *Giro d'Italia* (Tour of Italy), a three-week long bicycle race, attracts huge crowds along the route to see the cyclists speed past.

Italy's snow-covered mountain slopes attract skiers and snowboarders from all over the world. The most popular wintersport resorts are Cortina d'Ampezzo, Courmayeur, Livigno, and Sauze d'Oux.

 Web Search ▶▶

▶ http://www.calcioitalia.8m.com/home.htm
A site full of news and information about Italian soccer.

Daily Life and Religion

Daily life in Italy revolves around the family, but times are changing along with the traditional roles of men and women.

Daily life for women, especially in the major urban centers, has changed dramatically since the 1960s. Traditionally, men were the breadwinners and women looked after the home. Now, women no longer expect to spend their days at home. More women are staying in education to degree level and pursuing their own careers. Italian society is still male-dominated, but as more women work and study outside the home, Italian men have had to learn to share more of the home and family duties. Young Italians have readily accepted this cultural change.

The average lifespan of Italians is among the highest in the world. On average, women live more than six years longer than men. ▼

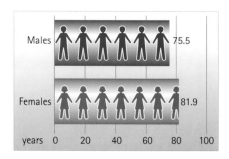

Males		75.5
Females		81.9
years	0 20 40 60 80 100	

◄◄ The area of the "Spanish Steps" in Rome, where some streets are closed off to traffic during the day so shoppers and tourists can walk freely. Pedestrianized areas are increasingly common in large Italian cities.

Food

Italian food has gained international popularity. Pizza, pasta dishes, rice-based risotto, and speciality meats such as Parma ham and salami are eaten all over the world. Italian cheeses are very popular, too—creamy ricotta made from sheep's milk, buffalo mozzarella made from buffalo milk, blue-veined gorgonzola, and hard parmesan.

Opening hours

Opening hours for shops vary from region to region, but most are open from 9:30 A.M. to 1:00 P.M. and 3:30 P.M. to 8:00 P.M., Monday to Saturday. A long break for lunch, lasting one or two hours, is common. Larger stores stay open all day. Very few shops and stores open on Sundays.

Religion

Vatican City, an independent state within Rome, is the capital of world Catholicism. Most of Italy's population is Roman Catholic. Church attendance throughout Italy has declined in recent years, but families still usually have their children baptized even if they are not regular church-goers. People in rural areas attend church most regularly.

The Turin Shroud

In Turin, the *Duomo*, the cathedral, holds a remarkable piece of cloth. It was thought by many Christians to be the sheet that Jesus Christ was wrapped in after being crucified. However, in 1988, scientific analysis showed that this "Turin Shroud" is no older than the 12th century.

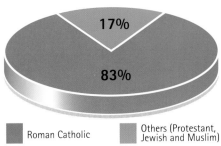

17%

83%

■ Roman Catholic   ■ Others (Protestant, Jewish and Muslim)

▲ More than 80 percent of Italians are Roman Catholic.

◄◄ Worshipers and tourists mingle outside the cathedral in Siena. Most cities and large towns have beautiful historic churches and cathedrals.

Web Search ►►

► http://www.vatican.va
The official Vatican Web site.

Arts and Media

Italy has one of the richest artistic and cultural heritages of any country. It has produced many of the world's greatest artists, sculptors, and composers.

The Renaissance period, from around 1450 to 1700, when all forms of art blossomed across Europe, was centered on Italy. During this period, the Mona Lisa, probably the world's best-known painting, was created by the Italian artist, scientist, engineer, and inventor, Leonardo da Vinci. One of the most famous statues, David, was created by the sculptor Michelangelo. Galleries around the world display the works of these and many other Italian Renaissance artists, including Raphael, Bellini, Titian, Caravaggio, Tintoretto, and Botticelli.

TV Broadcast Stations
(total 358)

☐ = 10 Stations

Radio Broadcast Stations
(total 4,709)

☐ = 100 Stations

▲ Italians have a wide choice of local, regional, and national broadcasters as well as satellite channels.

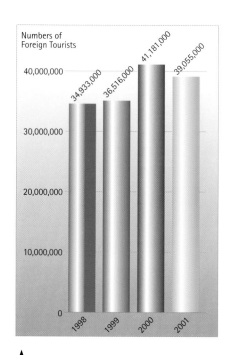

Numbers of Foreign Tourists

34,933,000 (1998)
36,516,000 (1999)
41,181,000 (2000)
39,055,000 (2001)

▲ Italy is one of the world's most popular tourist destinations. Visitors come from every continent for beach vacations, sightseeing, and winter sports.

24

Italians dress up for *Carnevale*, a major celebration that takes place in Venice each year to mark the beginning of the Christian festival of Lent. ▶▶

Opera and music

Italy is the home of opera. There are opera houses in all regions, including the world-famous La Scala in Milan. Musical works by Italian composers including Verdi, Puccini, Monteverdi, Rossini, and Vivaldi are regularly performed all over the world. One of the best-known opera singers today is the Italian tenor, Luciano Pavarotti.

Movies and film

Italian movies are renowned for being artistic and thought-provoking films. The best-known and most successful Italian film directors include Federico Fellini, Roberto Rossellini, Luchino Visconti, Pier Paulo Pasolini, Vittorio de Sica, and Bernardo Bertolucci. In the 1960s, Sergio Leone made a number of popular western movies that became known as "spaghetti westerns."

The Media

Italian broadcasting was controlled by the government and heavily influenced by the church until the 1970s, when privately owned radio or television stations were allowed. Hundreds of new radio and television stations sprang up. A number of television channels, radio stations, and newspapers are owned by one of Italy's most prominent politicians, Silvio Berlusconi, who was elected prime minister of Italy in 1994 and again in 2001. Most Italian newspapers are regional or focused on a particular city.

 Overseas visitors

Italy is the fourth most popular tourist destination in the world after France, the U.S., and Spain. Many visitors from northern Europe come by road, via tunnels through the Alps.

 Web Search ▶▶

▶ http://www.operabase.com
A Web site full of information about opera, including Italian opera.

▶ http://www.museionline.it
Information about museums in Italy.

Government

Italy has several different police forces. Most crimes are dealt with by the *Polizia*, the state police force. The *Carabinieri* is a military-style force that deals with a variety of crimes, including the activities of criminal organizations such as the Mafia. The *Vigili Urbani* deal with traffic and parking offenses. There is also a force called the *Guardia di Finanza* that deals with only financial crimes such as fraud.

After World War II, Italy's monarchy was abolished, and its constitution rewritten to ensure that it would be ruled not by a king, queen, or dictator, but by a democratically elected government.

The Italian parliament is bicameral (it has two houses). The upper house is the Senate, with 315 senators. The lower house is the Chamber of Deputies, with 630 members. Senators and deputies are elected by the people for a period of up to five years. Politics in Italy is more turbulent than in most other European countries. Italy has had more than 50 different governments since it became a democratic republic in 1946.

Provinces and Territories

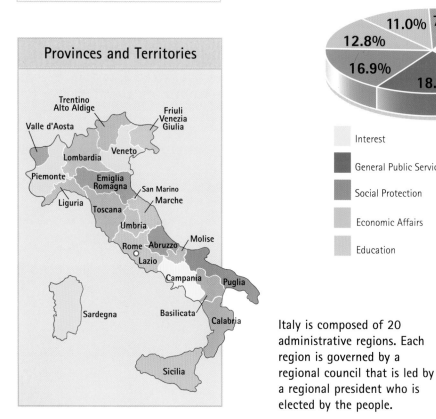

4.8% 3.5% 2.8% 0.5% Housing and community amenities

0.5% Environmental protection

11.0% 7.6%

12.8%

16.9%

18.9% 20.7%

Interest

General Public Services   Health

Social Protection   Public Order and Safety

Economic Affairs   Defense

Education   Recreation, Culture, and Religion

▲ A high proportion of government spending goes toward health, education, and public services, giving Italians a high standard of living.

Italy is composed of 20 administrative regions. Each region is governed by a regional council that is led by a regional president who is elected by the people.

26

The President

The head of state, the president, is elected to a seven-year term by an Electoral College made up of the Senate, the Chamber of Deputies, and representatives of regional councils. The president has a wide range of powers. He or she can call elections, dissolve parliament, and appoint the prime minister. The president also leads the High Council of the Magistracy, which guarantees the independence of the legal system.

Government

The national government consists of the Council of Ministers led by the prime minister. At a more local level, there are 20 regions. Five of them (Sicily, Sardinia, Valle d'Aosta, Trentino Alto Adige, and Friuli Venezia Giulia) have more autonomy than the others. Each region is divided into several provinces. At an even more local level, each province is divided into communes.

▲ A view overlooking most of Vatican City toward the historic center of Rome. Vatican City was made an independent state in 1929. It has its own government and diplomats.

Web Search ►►

► http://www.italyemb.org/government.htm
Web site of the Italian government.

► http://www.economist.com/countries/Italy
Information about Italy's politics and economics from The Economist *magazine.*

Place in the World

DATABASE

Chronology of Historical Events up to 1800

1000 B.C.
The Etruscans begin living in Italy

700s B.C. to A.D. 476
The Roman Empire; in A.D. 330, the Empire was divided into East and West halves

A.D. 485
Attila the Hun invades Italy

553
The Roman Empire is reunited by the Byzantine emperor, Justinian

800
Charlemagne, King of France, is crowned emperor of the Romans

814
Charlemagne dies; his son, Louis I, divides up the kingdom

962
The Holy Roman Empire begins under Otto the Great, King of Germany

1519
King Charles I of Spain becomes Emperor Charles V of the Holy Roman Empire

1700s
Spanish rule declines and Italy comes under Austrian rule

1796
Napoleon of France expels the Austrian rulers

Italy was once at the heart of an empire that stretched across most of Europe. The Roman Empire introduced more advanced roads, buildings, bridges, and town planning, plus a common language (Latin) and legal system to the countries it conquered.

Today, Italy still plays an important role in European affairs. It is one of the founding members of the European Union (EU). More than half of its international trade is with other European countries, mainly Germany, France, Spain, and The Netherlands. The government continues to promote the development of the poorer southern region of Italy to reduce unemployment, increase prosperity, and narrow the gap with the wealthier north.

St. Angelo's Castle in Rome was originally the burial place of Roman Emperor Hadrian. Then, it became part of Vatican City. Now, Italy wants to claim it back as part of its history. ▶▶

28

International links

In addition to its membership of the European Union, Italy takes part in many international organizations including the United Nations (UN), UNESCO (the United Nations Educational, Scientific and Cultural Organization), the International Olympic Committee (IOC), the World Trade Organization, and the World Health Organization (WHO).

A comparison of the value and major items of Italy's exports and imports. Income from tourism helps keep the country's trade profitable. ▶▶

EXPORTS

$272 billion (engineering products, textiles, clothing, machinery, vehicles, transportation equipment, chemicals, food, beverages, tobacco, minerals, metals)

IMPORTS

$250 billion (engineering products, chemicals, transportation equipment, energy products, minerals, metals, textiles, clothing, food, beverages, tobacco)

DATABASE

Chronology of Historical Events from 1800

1861
Italy's states are unified, forming modern Italy

1871
Rome becomes Italy's capital

1922
Benito Mussolini becomes Italy's dictatorial leader

1936
Italy forms an alliance with Nazi Germany

1940–41
Italy declares war on Britain, France, the U.S., and the USSR (Soviet Union)

1943
The Allies invade Italy, and Mussolini is overthrown

1945
Mussolini is executed

1946
Italy becomes a republic

1970
Divorce is legalized

1978
Abortion is legalized

1984
Roman Catholicism ceases to be the state religion

2002
The Euro replaces the Lira as currency

◀◀ The annual children's international book fair in Bologna is the largest of its kind in the world.

Area:
116,323 sq miles (301,278 sq km) including Sicily and Sardinia

Population size:
57,423,000

Capital city:
Rome (population 4,000,000)

Other major cities:
Milan (pop. 1,465,000),
Naples (pop. 1,300,000),
Turin (pop. 1,000,000),
Palermo (pop. 730,000),
Genoa (pop. 640,000),
Bologna (pop. 400,000)

Longest river:
Po (400 miles [650 km])

Biggest lakes:
Lake Garda (143 sq mi [370 sq km])
Lake Maggiore
(81 sq mi [212 sq km])
Lake Como (56 sq mi [146 sq km])

Highest mountain:
Monte Bianco/Mont Blanc (15,623 feet [4,807 m]). The mountain straddles the French-Italian border, with the summit in France. Highest mountain completely within Italy: Gran Paradiso (13,198 feet [4,061 m])

Currency:
1 Euro = 100 cents
$1 = .78 Euros approximately

Flag:
Three equal vertical bands of green (flagpole side), white, and red

Languages:
Italian (official), German, French, Rhaeto-Romanic, Sardinian, Slovene

Major resources:
Natural gas, pumice, feldspar, aluminium, potash, asbestos

Major exports:
Engineering products, textiles, clothing, footwear, machinery, vehicles, transportation equipment, chemicals, food, beverages, tobacco, minerals, metals

National holidays and major events:
January 1: New Year's Day
January 6: Epiphany
Easter Monday: Pasquetta
April 25: Liberation Day
May 1: Labor Day
August 15: Assumption of the Blessed Virgin Mary
November 1: All Souls' Day
December 8: Immaculate Conception of the Blessed Virgin Mary
December 25: Christmas Day
December 26: St. Stephen's Day

Religions:
Roman Catholic: 83 percent,
Others (including Protestant, Jewish, and Muslim): 17 percent

Glossary

AGRICULTURE
Farming the land, including plowing, planting, raising crops, and raising animals.

BIRTH RATE
The number of babies born in a year compared to a set number of people, usually the number of babies born per 1,000 people in the population.

CLIMATE
The long-term weather in an area.

CULTURE
The beliefs, ideas, knowledge, and customs of a group of people, or the group of people themselves.

ECONOMY
A country's finances, including imports, exports, and government spending.

EMPIRE
A group of colonies ruled by a single country.

EXPORTS
Products, resources, or goods sold to other countries.

GOVERNMENT
A group of people who manage a country, deciding on laws, raising taxes, and organizing health, education, transportation, and other national systems and services.

GROSS DOMESTIC PRODUCT
The value of all goods and services produced by a nation in a year.

IMPORTS
Products, resources, or goods brought into the country.

LITERACY
The ability to read and write.

LITERACY RATE
The percentage of the population who can read and write.

MANUFACTURING
Making large numbers of the same things by hand or, more commonly, by machine.

POPULATION
All of the people who live in a city, country, region, or other area.

POPULATION DENSITY
The average number of people living in each square mile of a city, country, region, or other area.

REPUBLIC
An independent country whose head of state is an elected president.

RESOURCES
Materials that can be used to make goods or electricity, or to generate income for a country or region.

RURAL
Having the qualities of the countryside, with a low population density.

URBAN
Having the qualities of a city, with a high population density.

Index

Adriatic Sea 7, 13
agriculture 12, 14, 30
Alps 6
Apennines 6, 7
art 4, 24

Berlusconi, Silvio 25
Bologna 29, 30
broadcasting 25

climate 4, 7
Colosseum 11, 24
currency 29, 30

Dolomites 6

earthquakes 6
education 18

farming 12
fashion 4, 15
festivals 20, 25, 30
fishing 12, 13
Florence 4
food 4, 22

Genoa 30
government 26, 27

Herculaneum 7, 24
holidays 30

immigration 9
industry 14

Lake Como 30
Lake Garda 30

Lake Maggiore 24, 30
language 8, 30
Leonardo da Vinci 4
Liguria 21
literacy 18, 19

Mafia 26
Mediterranean Sea 7
Michelangelo 24
minerals 15, 30
Monte Bianco (Mont Blanc) 6, 30
Monte Cervino (the Matterhorn) 6
Montessori schools 18
Mt. Etna 7
Mt. Gran Paradiso 30
Mt. Stromboli 7
Mt. Vesuvius 7
mountains 6, 7, 30
movies 25
music 25
Mussolini, Benito 29

Naples 30
natural resources 14, 30
newspapers 25

opera 25

Palio, the 20
Parma 13
Pavarotti, Luciano 25
Pisa, Leaning Tower of 24
police 26
Pompeii 7, 24
Pope 4, 29
population 8, 9, 10, 11, 30
provinces 26, 27

Puglia 11

railroads 16, 17
rainfall 7
religion 23, 30
resources 14, 30
river Arno 4
river Po 7, 30
rivers 4, 7, 30
roads 16, 17
Roman Empire 28
Rome 9, 11, 17, 20, 22, 28, 29, 30

Sardinia 4, 13
Sicily 4, 13
Siena 8, 23
spaghetti westerns 25
sport 20, 21

tourism 14, 16, 24, 25
trade 28, 29
transportation 16, 17
Turin 22, 30
Turin Shroud 22
Tuscany 11, 12, 24
Tyrrhenian Sea 13

Umbria 11, 24

Vatican City 4, 23, 27, 28
Venice 10, 20, 24, 25
volcanoes 6, 7

weather 7
wildlife 6
winemaking 12